essentials

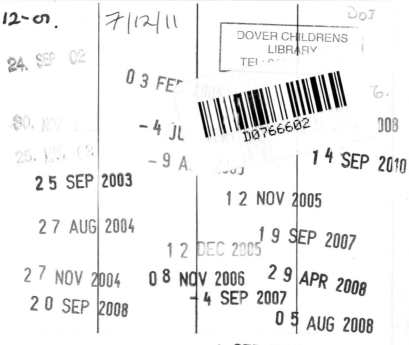

12-09.   7/12/11   DOT

24. SEP 02

03 FEB   6.

30. NOV   -4 JL   D0766602   008

25. NOV 09   -9 A   1 4 SEP 2010

2 5 SEP 2003

                               1 2 NOV 2005

2 7 AUG 2004

                1 2 DEC 2005 1 9 SEP 2007

2 7 NOV 2004   0 8 NOV 2006   2 9 APR 2008

2 0 SEP 2008   -4 SEP 2007

                                0 5 AUG 2008

                -4 SEP 2007

Books should be returned or renewed by the
last date stamped above

372·632.

ADAMS, Ken

Help your 7-11 year old

spell well

Awarded for excellence
to Arts & Libraries

Parents' essentials – friendly books for busy parents
to help their children fulfil their potential.

For full details please send for a free copy of the latest catalogue.
See back cover for address.

Help Your 7–11 Year Old Spell Well

Ken Adams

PARENTS' ESSENTIALS

Published in 2001 by
How To Books Ltd, 3 Newtec Place,
Magdalen Road, Oxford OX4 1RE, United Kingdom
Tel: (01865) 793806   Fax: (01865) 248780
email: info@howtobooks.co.uk
www.howtobooks.co.uk

British Library Cataloguing in Publication Data.
A catalogue record for this book is available from
the British Library.

Cover design by Shireen Nathoo Design
Produced for How To Books by Deer Park Productions
Typeset by PDQ Typesetting, Newcastle-under-Lyme, Staffordshire
Printed and bound in Great Britain by The Baskerville Press Ltd.

NOTE: The material contained in this book is set out in good faith
for general guidance and no liability can be accepted for loss or
expense incurred as a result of relying in particular circumstances
on statements made in the book. Laws and regulations are complex
and liable to change, and readers should check the current position
with the relevant authorities before making personal arrangements.

ESSENTIALS *is an imprint of*
How To Books

Contents

Preface

This book seeks to eradicate spelling difficulties in the primary age group. It is an age at which good teaching, or help at home, can ensure that a child grows into an adult who is competent and confident with spelling.

English spelling is difficult. There are many rules for beginnings, middles and endings, but also many exceptions which need to be learnt separately. This book includes all the major rules and exceptions and lays out spelling words in structured groups to make learning easy. Also, words have been chosen that are appropriate to the age group, although some harder words have been included to stretch the faster learner.

Ken Adams

1 Learning Spelling by Structural Methods

Many studies in psychology have shown that if learning is made meaningful for the learner, then that learning is much easier. Meaningful means both relating subjects like spelling to real-life understanding. For example, relating a word like 'monkey' to its real-life image helps both reading and spelling. Even silent letter words like lamb can be easily remembered if a child can visualise the silent letter floating above its position in the word:

```
              b
    l a m    is   l a m b

         u
    b  o y   is   b u o y
```

So, words that do not fit into a pattern can be remembered easily simply by emphasising where they differ from that pattern.

For the great majority of words, however, their spelling either fits into a pattern or can be closely related to some structural pattern, such as phonics. The structure of phonic words, for example, relates closely to the use of consonants with short vowels like 'a' for apple, 'e' for egg and so on; the 'shon' sound at the end of words is either represented by '-tion' or by '-sion'.

STEP-WISE LEARNING

As with all learning, spelling is best learnt by progressing from considering simple structures and basic sounds, to the more complex. Initially, it is important to learn the sounds of the alphabet, because these provide a basis for phonic word building. A short vowel combined with two consonants is a simple three-letter word:

e g g

c a t

Many words are built on phonic structures, and these are relatively easy to learn to spell:

b a t   b a t t l e   c o t   c a n   c a n n o t

b a t t i n g   s c o t   c a n e

Moving from learning simple structures to more complex ones is by small steps. This is termed step-wise or sequenced learning. It moves the learner further along a path, building new knowledge on what is already in the learner's memory. However, in spelling there are many paths that can be taken, and many ways to link patterns as knowledge is built up. This book follows one particular path after a phonic basis has been established.

The spelling groups in different chapters have been used successfully by the author with a wide variety of ages and abilities.

'GOOD' SPELLERS AND 'BAD' SPELLERS

There is a school of thought that believes that good readers become good spellers. Many of those who read early also become very good spellers, as they seem to be able to instinctively recognise patterns within text. However, this is not always the case. Two girls of 9 years and 11 years whom I taught were excellent readers. They read widely and with great interest; but they were very bad spellers. It was only when they were taught spelling as a separate subject, and in a constructive way, that their spelling 'caught up'.

DIFFICULTIES IN SPELLING

Many of the sections in this book have been organised so that word groups with similar patterns have been placed together. This considerably aids learning, especially if the overall rules are stressed. For example, it helps if the learner knows that with many single syllable words the ending consonant doubles – sit becomes sitting, trap becomes trapped. Following from this, the learner then has to recognise exceptions – hope becomes hoping. Such a systematised system aids recall and can help to turn even bad spellers into good spellers.

2 A Basis for Spelling: Phonics

THE ALPHABET – SHORT VOWELS

a for apple

e for egg

i for insect

o for orange

u for umbrella

Using these, simple phonic words can be constructed:

p - i - n

c - a - t

d - o - g

j - u - g

l - e - g

Try these

Get your child to unjumble these words:

(1) ath, tca, tam, gra, cpa, anc, anf, anr, nam, abg.

(2) teb, ste, dre, def, nhe, etj, tle, enm, tve, tew, ety.

(3) pdi, inp, dri, sni, piz, imv, its, ibr.

(4) tco, ocd, ogc, poc, xoc, toh, ohp, gho, toj, jbo, olt, blo, bmo, sbo.

(5)   ucb, puc, tuc, ddu, gdu, nuf, ung, thu, bhu, dum, unn.

DOUBLE BLENDS AS BEGINNINGS

These include beginnings to words like:

br-, bl-, cr-, cl-, dr-, fl-, fr-, gl-, gr-, pl-, pr-, sc-, sl-, sm-, sp-, st-, tr-, th-, sh-, ch-.

Some words with these double blends are:

b l o t	b r a t	c r a b
c l u b	d r u m	f l a t
f r o g	g l u m	g r i p
p r a m	p l u m	s t o p
s p o t	s l a p	c a n
s m o g	t r a p	t h e n
c h i p	s h o p	

These words are very simply built on the basic phonic structure.

Try these

Join the correct beginning with the correct ending using a pencil line:

Beginning	Ending
s h	- a b
c h	- u b
t h	- u m
b l	- a t
b r	- o p
c l	- o t
c r	- i p
d r	- e n
f l	- i p
f r	- a t
g r	- o g
p r	- o t
p l	- a n
s t	- a p
s p	- o g
s l	- o p
s c	- a m
s m	- a p
t r	- u m

MIDDLES

There are two very common middles that are easy to learn as spellings – 'oo' and 'ee'. These give rise to a series of words whose spellings are usually easily remembered:

m o o n	s p o o n	s o o n
l o o t	n o o n	s t o o p
s t o o l	c o o l	s h o o t
b o o t	h o o t	s c o o t
m o o d	r o o t	t o o t
f o o l	t o o t h	f o o d

and,

f e e t	m e e t	b e e t
b e e n	h e e l	s e e n
f e e l	k e e n	j e e p
l e e k	s e e k	t e e t h
w e e d	f e e d	s p e e d
s t e e l	s h e e t	s t e e p

Try these

Put -oo- or -ee- in the space to make a recognisable word:

m _ _ n

s p _ _ n

s _ _ k

n _ _ n

w _oo_ d

b _ee_ n

r _oo_ t

j _ee_ p

s p _ee_ d

m _oo_ d

l _oo_ t

h _ee_ l

w _oo_ l

c _oo_ l

TRIPLE BLENDS

Early stumbling blocks with spelling often occur with beginnings that include spr, spl, str and scr.

Words with triple blend beginnings

s p r a t	s p r i g	s p l i t
s p l a s h	s t r a p	s t r i p
s c r a m		

3 Important Endings

PLURALS

There is a wide variety of plural endings apart from simply adding on s. For example, changes to words ending in y, -es endings, -f endings and plurals by vowel change or by no change at all.

Adding an -s

home	homes
girl	girls
boy	boys
wheel	wheels
balloon	balloons
ribbon	ribbons
book	books
hand	hands

There are many more. If the word ends in -e (e.g. home) it is safe to add an -s.

Words ending in y

This includes two very important rules.

1. If there is a vowel before the y, then the plural adds an -s:

key	keys

m o n k e y	m o n k e y s
t r a y	t r a y s
p l a y	p l a y s

2. If there is a consonant before the y, the y becomes -ies:

b a b y	b a b i e s
b o d y	b o d i e s
f l y	f l i e s
f a m i l y	f a m i l i e s
l a d y	l a d i e s
p o n y	p o n i e s
s k y	s k i e s
s t o r y	s t o r i e s

Try these

Write the plurals of these words:

t r a y   _____

l a d y   _____

w h e e l   _____

k e y   _____

fly   _____

story   _____

play   _____

boy   _____

baby   _____

sky   _____

monkey   _____

Plurals that add -es

ben c̲h̲	benches
lun c̲h̲	lunches
bu s̲	buses
bru s̲h̲	brushes
cra s̲h̲	crashes
tor c̲h̲	torches
cro s̲s̲	crosses
pa s̲s̲	passes
fo x̲	foxes
bu s̲h̲	bushes

There are others that can be added to this list, but these are the main words for this age group.

Plurals from -f or -fe endings

r o o f	r o o f s
c l i f f	c l i f f s
h a l f	h a l v e s
k n i f e	k n i v e s
l o a f	l o a v e s
l e a f	l e a v e s
l i f e	l i v e s
w i f e	w i v e s
w o l f	w o l v e s
y o u r s e l f	y o u r s e l v e s
s c a r f	s c a r v e s (or s c a r f s)
h o o f	h o o v e s (or h o o f s)
d w a r f	d w a r v e s (or d w a r f s)

-o ending plurals

r a d i o	r a d i o s
r a t i o	r a t i o s

(when -o has a vowel in front)

k i l o	k i l o s

photo	photos
piano	pianos
zero	zeros
echo	echoes
hero	heroes
no	noes
volcano	volcanoes
tomato	tomatoes
potato	potatoes

'No change' plurals

These are the same whether plural or singular:

fish	sheep	deer

Those *only* in the plural are:

cattle	scissors

Vowel changes

foot	feet
man	men
tooth	teeth
woman	women
goose	geese
mouse	mice

Try these

Put in the plurals of these words:

b u s   _____

r o o f   _____

k i l o   _____

f o x   _____

l e a f   _____

m a n   _____

m o u s e   _____

w o m a n   _____

c r a s h   _____

b u s h   _____

w o l f   _____

g o o s e   _____

p o t a t o   _____

4 Simple Word Middles and Some Endings

'ai'/'ay'/'ey' sounds

c h a i n	r a i l	r a i n	t r a i n
w a i t	s n a i l	s a i l	f a i l

These have the same two vowel (diphthong) sounds as:

d a y	c r a y o n	p l a y	p r a y
t r a y	d e l a y	p l a y e r	p r a y e r
t h e y	o b e y		

'ou'/'ow' sounds

a b o u t	c l o u d	l o u d	r o u n d
a l o u d	g r o u n d	h o u r	s o u n d

and

b r o w n	c l o w n	d r o w n	f l o w e r
n o w	r o w (a noise)	t o w n	

'oi'/'oy' sounds

b o i l	j o i n	n o i s e	o i l
s o i l			

and

boy   joy   royal   toy

'ea'/'ai' sounds

bear   pear   tear   wear

air   chair   fair   hair

pair   stairs

'ear'/'er'/'ir'/'or'/'our'/'ur' sounds

earth   learn

verse   were   herd

bird   dirt   first   third

word   work   world   worm

worse

journey

burger   burn   church   hurt

murder   nurse   purse

'oo'/'ew'/'ue'/'ou'/'o'/'ui'/'wo'/'ough' sound (as in blue)

blew   drew   grew

blue

do   lose   move   who   remove

food   shoot   goose   choose

group   soup

through

fruit   juice   suit

to   too   two

'oh'/'oa'/'oe'/'ow'/'ew'/'ough' sound

boat   coach   coat   oak

road   soap   toast

toe

blow   snow   tow   yellow

though

sew

'a'/'au'/'aw'/'al' sound

call   fall   talk   walk

ball   chalk   hall   tall

wall

caught   daughter

drawing   lawn   paw   yawn

claw

'ee'/'ea'/'ie'/'ei' sound

leap

green   three   weed   sleep

field   niece   piece

shield

ceiling   weird

short 'i'/'ui' sound
mischief

building biscuit   guilt

long 'i'/'ie'/'igh'/'y'/'ei' sound
die   lie   tie

height   neither   either

light   sight   might

night   fight   high

fly   try   why   cry

'eer'/'ea' sounds
dear   ear   disappear   tear

hear   near   spear

cheer   steer

'eh'/'ie' sound
bread   breath   death

head   tread   health

pleasant

friend

short 'o'/'au'/'ou'/'ow'/'ach' sound

b e c a u s e   s a u s a g e   A u s t r a l i a

c o u g h   k n o w l e d g e

y a c h t

'oo'/'u' sounds

(a) c o u l d   s h o u l d   w o u l d

(b) d o u b l e   r o u g h   t o u g h

   y o u n g

'yew' sound

y e w   d e w   f e w   k n e w

n e w

y o u

Try these

(1) Use '<u>ai</u>', '<u>ay</u>', '<u>ey</u>', '<u>ou</u>', '<u>ow</u>' sounds to complete the correct words:

s n_____ l   c r _____ o n

a l_____ d   f l _____ e r

c l_____ d   p l _____ e r

w_____ t   g r _____ n d

c h_____ n

(2) Use 'oi', 'oy', 'ea', 'ai', and 'or' 'ur', 'ir' sounds to complete:

j _____ n   r _____ a l

s t_____ r s   l _____ r n

w_____ l d   c h_____ c h

b_____ g e r   f _____ s t

s n_____ l   m _____ d e r

(3) Use 'oo', sounds to complete:

d r_____   l _____ s e

c h_____ s e   s _____ p

t h r_____   j _____ c e

g r_____ p   r e m_____ v e

(4) Use 'oh', 'aw', 'ee' sounds to complete:

c _____ c h   b l _____

t _____   th _____

c h_____ l k   c _____ t

p _____ c e   g r _____ n

l _____ p   d r _____ i n g

(5) Use short 'o' sounds, short 'i' sounds, long 'i' sounds to complete:

h _____ t   b _____ i l d i n g

f _____ t   b e c_____ s e

s _____ s a g e   c _____ g h

n _____ t h e r   b i s c_____ t

_____ s t r a l i a

(6) Use 'eer', 'eh', 'yew' and 'u' sounds to complete:

b r_____ d   f r _____ n d

c h_____ r   c _____ l d

r _____ g h   h _____ r

k n_____   p l _____ s a n t

'Middles' are a difficult area. Learnt thoroughly they provide an excellent base on which many common spelling words can be built.

5 Useful Areas to Know About

This includes the spelling of days, numbers, months; the rule of 'i before e except after c'; silent letters and adding an ending to a consonant (for example, big, bigger, biggest).

DAYS, NUMBERS AND MONTHS

Particular difficulties in these areas include the spellings of 'eight', 'Wednesday', and 'February'. Otherwise, these spellings depend on practice, and usage in letters and writing. Below are most useful words in this area. The underlined letters need to be emphasised:

Days

M o n d a y　　T u e s d a y　　W e d n e s d a y

T h u r s d a y　　F r i d a y　　S a t u r d a y

S u n d a y

Numbers

O n e, t w o, t h r e e, f o u r, f i v e, s i x, s e v e n, e i g h t, n i n e, t e n, e l e v e n, t w e l v e, t h i r t e e n, f o u r t e e n, f i f t e e n, s i x t e e n, s e v e n t e e n, e i g h t e e n, n i n e t e e n, t w e n t y

Months

J a n u a r y, F e b r u a r y, M a r c h, A p r i l, M a y,

June, July, August, September, October,
November, December

'I BEFORE E EXCEPT AFTER C'
This rule applies in particular to the 'ee' sound.

Following the rule

chief	field	niece	piece
pier	priest	shield	
ceiling	receive	deceive	

Exceptions to the rule

seize	protein	species

OTHER 'IE' AND 'EI' WORDS

'ei' words

weigh	eight	rein	reign
vein	weight		
foreign			
either	height	neither	

'ie' words

handkerchief		series mischief
died	tied	lied
friend		

patient

view

SILENT LETTERS

'h' heir   honest   hour

'g' gnome   gnat

'e' foreign   reign

'k' knee   kneel   knife   knit

knight   knock   know   unknown

'p' psychology   pterodactyl

'w' wrap   wreck   wriggle   wrist

wrong   write   answer   sword

'u' biscuit   buoy

'b' thumb   comb   lamb

'd' Wednesday

6 Endings for Words

ADDING AN ENDING AFTER A CONSONANT

Does the consonant double at the end of a word? is the question. There are some hard and fast rules to this question, some patterns and, therefore, groups to learn about.

The consonants doubled with short words (single syllable)

b a t	b a t t e d	
b e d	b e d d i n g	
b e g	b e g g e d	b e g g a r
c l a p	c l a p p e d	
d r o p	d r o p p e d	d r o p p i n g
f a t	f a t t e r	f a t t e s t
f i t	f i t t e r	f i t t e s t
h o p	h o p p e d	h o p p i n g
r u b	r u b b e r	r u b b e d
s a d	s a d d e r	
s i t	s i t t i n g	
s t o p	s t o p p e d	s t o p p i n g
t r a p	t r a p p e d	

Exceptions

A long vowel sound results in **one** consonant before the ending:

hope   hoping

shone   shining

stare   staring

'w', 'x' and 'y' do not double

saw   sawed

fry   fried   frying

stay   staying   stayed

tax   taxed

Two vowel words do not double

beat   beating

creep   creeping

heat   heating

hoot   hooted

leap   leaping

sail   sailed   sailing

sleep   sleeping

Exception

quiz   quizzed

quit   quitted

Two or three consonant words do not double

f a s t	f a s t e r	f a s t e s t
t u r n	t u r n e d	
r e a c h	r e a c h e d	
r u s h	r u s h e d	
w a t c h	w a t c h i n g	

Emphasising different parts of the word ending in a consonant affects whether the ending is doubled or not.

Stressing the last part of the word doubles the consonant.

a d m i t	a d m i t t e d
b e g i n	b e g i n n i n g
f o r g e t	f o r g e t t i n g
f o r g o t	f o r g o t t e n
q u a r r e l	q u a r r e l l e d
r e g r e t	r e g r e t t e d

Where the emphasis is on the first part of the word, there is **no** doubling:

b e n e f i t	b e n e f i t e d
c a r p e t	c a r p e t e d
c r i c k e t	c r i c k e t e r
g a l l o p	g a l l o p e d

gossip	gossiping
hiccup	hiccuped
letter	lettering
profit	profited
target	targeted

Words ending in w, x or y in this section do not double the consonants:

allow	allowed
destroy	destroyed
relax	relaxed

Exceptions

kidnap	kidnapped
handicap	handicapped
input	inputted

If the ending (suffix) begins with a consonant, it usually just adds on:

drunken	drunkenness
mean	meanness
commit	commitment
develop	development
equip	equipment

govern   government

paper   paperback

Changing and dropping vowels affects the addition of an ending:

curious   curiosity

enter   entrance

exclaim   exclamation

hunger   hungry

proclaim   proclamation

pronounce   pronunciation

compel   compulsion

expel   expulsion

humour   humorous

Try these spelling tests
This chapter has thrown up many difficulties, so the tests are fairly extensive. It is best to allow adequate time for a learner to absorb this section.

Add -ed to and -ing to these words:

	-ed	-ing
bat	_____	_____
slap	_____	_____

	-ed	*-ing*
h o o t	_____	_____
s t a y	_____	_____
t u r n	_____	_____
q u i z	_____	_____
e q u i p	_____	_____
q u a r r e l	_____	_____
s t e w	_____	_____
t a x	_____	_____
b l a n k e t	_____	_____
g a l l o p	_____	_____
h a p p e n	_____	_____
k i d n a p	_____	_____
f a s t	_____	_____
s t a r e	_____	_____
f r y	_____	_____
t r y	_____	_____
s i p	_____	_____

	-ed	-ing
d r o p	_____	_____
t a r g e t	_____ ,	_____
d e s t r o y	_____	_____
r e l a x	_____	_____

Make the word by adding the ending:

commit + ment = _____

embarrass + ment = _____

pocket + full = _____

foot + note = _____

curious + ity = _____

disaster + ous = _____

enter + ance = _____

generous + ity = _____

compel + sion = _____

humour + ous = _____

7 More Endings

ENDINGS IN -L

All becomes a*l*

almost already alright welcome

Full becomes *ful*

beautiful careful helpful

painful wonderful cupful

spoonful

Some words add on -ly to an l ending

accidentally actually

eventually generally

Other words add on -ly and *leave out* the l ending

completely desperately extremely

fortunately friendly immediately

lonely lovely quickly

quietly

-y ending becomes -i

busily greedily

hungrily happily

necessarily readily

-ic ending adds -ally

basically   comically   terrifically

Exception

public →   publicly

-ble → -bly, -ple → -ply

capably   favourably

irritably   possibly

supply   terribly

valuably   simply

Exceptions

truly   wholly   fully

Adding an ending with a vowel doubles the -l

cancel   cancelled

expel   expelled

label   labelled

quarrel   quarrelled

signal   signalled

travel   travelled

Exception

appealed	appealing

Adding a consonant – keeps a single 'l'

compel	compulsion
expel	expulsion
quarrel	quarrelsome
rival	rivalry
wilful	wilfulness

ENDINGS AFTER VOWELS

Dropping an -e

adore	adorable
argue	arguable
believe	believable
cure	curable
describe	describable
excite	excitable
love	lovable
remove	removable
change	changing
notice	noticing
give	giving

Exceptions

changeable	manageable
noticeable	likeable
conspire	conspiracy
pirate	piracy
response	responsible
adore	adoring
argue	arguing
become	becoming
believe	believing
come	coming
drive	driving
excite	exciting
forgive	forgiving

There are many others in this section.

Exceptions

dye	dyeing
queue	queueing
see	seeing
eye	eyeing

Keeping the -e

careful	peaceful
useful	
accurate	accurately
approximate	approximately
complete	completely
love	lovely

Exception: true   truly

achieve	achievement
arrange	arrangement
excite	excitement
replace	replacement

Exception: argue   argument

No change

	-ed	-ing
echo	echoed	echoing
ski	skied	skiing

-ABLE AND -IBLE WORD ENDINGS

There are no hard and fast rules for these – learn well!

-able

acceptable	advisable
available	believable
comfortable	considerable
desirable	eatable
excitable	inflammable
irritable	likeable
loveable	reliable
suitable	usable
variable	

-ible

digestible	combustible
divisible	inaudible
indelible	indigestible
invincible	legible
perceptible	possible
responsible	reversible
sensible	visible

Try these

Combine the words and part-words:

beauty + -full = _____

w o n d e r + -f u l l =   _____

b u s y + -l y =   _____

t e r r i b l e + -y   _____

s i m p l e + -y =   _____

c a n c e l + -e d =   _____

c o m p e l + -s i o n =   _____

a d o r e + -a b l e =   _____

a r g u e + - i n g =   _____

l i k e + -a b l e =   _____

f o r g i v e + -i n g =   _____

c a r e + -f u l l =   _____

l o v e + -l y =   _____

t r u e + -l y =   _____

e x c i t e + -m e n t =   _____

e c h o + - e d =   _____

l o v e + -a b l e =   _____

r e s p o n s e + - i b l e =   _____

s e n s e + -i b l e =   _____

8 Even More Endings

The variety in endings seems to go on for ever.

-ce/-se

noun	verb
advice	advise
practice	practise

-ceed, -cess, -eeding, -ede, -ssion

exceed	proceed	succeed
excess	process	success
exceeding	proceeding	succeeding
recede	concede	precede
concession	recession	

-acle, -ical, -icle

chemical	comical	geographical
medical	mechanical	physical
vertical	typical	
spectacle	tentacle	miracle
article	icicle	vehicle

-er nouns

baker	butcher	buyer
computer	character	cooker

daughter   driver   farmer

fighter   gardener   helicopter

lawyer   lender   loser

master   murder

-or nouns

author   conjuror   conqueror

councillor   counsellor   debtor

doctor   editor   emperor

governor   meteor   professor

solicitor   spectator   tractor

-re words

centimetre   centre   fibre

litre   metre   millimetre

theatre

-our words

behaviour   colour   flavour

hour   humour   neighbour

our

-ary, -ery, -ory, -ry, -ury endings

imaginary   military   primary

secondary	solitary	stationary (still)
summary	voluntary	temporary
burglary	dictionary	February
library	salary	secretary
celery	cemetary	cookery
grocery	jewellery	mystery
surgery	trickery	stationery (paper)
advisory	compulsory	satisfactory
factory	history	laboratory
lavatory	memory	territory
dairy	hairy	
hurry	marry	worry
chemistry	country	fairy
poetry	sentry	rivalry
century	fury	treasury

-ion, -sion, -ssim, -cian, -tian, endings

accommodation		attention
civilisation	competition	condition
description	education	fraction
imagination	nation	occupation
perception	population	position

prescription	probation	punctuation
reception	rejection	revolution
solution	station	suggestion
collision	comprehension	
occasion	pension	
admission	permission	profession
electrician	magician	musician
optician	politician	

-ous, -eous, -ious endings

dangerous	enormous	famous
jealous	marvellous	nervous
ridiculous	treacherous	conspicuous
deciduous	mischievous	
humorous	vigorous	
hideous	miscellaneous	
spontaneous	simultaneous	
advantageous	courageous	
envious	mysterious	
curious	previous	serious
atrocious	gracious	precious
suspicious	vicious	

anxious   conscious   superstitious

-ant, -ent words

abundant   constant   distant

extravagant   instant   pleasant

pregnant   significant   vacant

currant (fruit) descendant   peasant

pheasant   plant   restaurant

transplant

cement   comment   element

garment   torment

absent   content   current
                                    (flow of air etc)

decent   different   efficient

evident   excellent   frequent

magnificent   obedient   patient

permanent   recent   transparent

subsequent

ascent   continent   equivalent

patient   president

cement   frequent   repent

-ance words

abundance	appearance	disturbance
entrance	glance	performance
resistance	romance	substance

-ence words

difference	evidence	existence
licence	obedience	occurrence
preference	presence	pretence

-ense words

condense	dense	expense
suspense	tense	

-ancy/-ency

buoyancy	infancy	vacancy
deficiency	emergency	frequency

-ise words

practise	promise	
advertise	advise	
disguise	exercise	surprise
agonise	criticise	
civilisation	fertiliser	
standardisation		

analyse   paralyse

-y, -ey, -ie, -ee endings
ecstasy   happy

cry   sky

prophecy   prophesy
(noun)   (verb)

key   money

grey   prey (bird of)

zombie

degree   reference   employee

-efy/-ify
liquefy

rarefy   rarefied

crucify   horrify   terrify

crucified   horrified   terrified

crucifixion

-ed/-t endings
learn   learnt/learned

name   named

burn   burnt/burned

dream   dreamt/dreamed

l e n d   l e n t

s p e n d   s p e n t

Try these

(1) Put the correct endings – <u>acle</u>, <u>ical</u>, <u>icle</u>

c h e m_____   v e h_____

t e n t_____   m i r_____

a r t_____   s p e c t_____

(2) Choose -or, -re, -er, or -our endings

b u t c h_____   a u t h_____   m e t_____

p r o f e s s_____   d o c t_____   l a w y_____

c h a r a c t_____   c e n t_____   h u m_____

c o l_____   e m p e r_____   h e l i c o p t____

s o l i c i t_____

(3) Choose -ary, -ery, -ory, -ry, or ury endings

c e l_____   b u r g l_____   f a c t_____

h i s t_____   c h e m i s t_____

c e n t_____   l i b r_____   d i c t i o n_____

(4) Put on -tion, -sion, -ssion, -cian or -tian endings

r e c e p_____   s t a_____

c o l l i_____   o c c a_____

a d m i_____   m a g i_____

(5) Add -ous, -eous or -ious.

r i d i c u l_____   a d v a n t a g____

c u r_____   a n x_____

(6) Put in -ant, -ent, -ance, -ence, -ancy, -ency

p l e a s_____   a b s_____

o b e d i_____   p a t i_____

r e s t a u r_____   g a r m_____

e v i d_____   e x p_____

v a c_____   f r e q u_____

a b u n d_____

(7) Put in -ise, -y, -ey, -ie, -ee, -efy/-ify, -ed/-t

e c s t a s_____   z o m b_____   a n a_____

d e g r_____   t e r r i f_____   a g o n_____

p a r a l_____   m o n_____

9 More Beginnings and Middles

USING I OR Y

biology	diet
biscuit	cinema
tickle	
cycle	typist
tyre	
syrup	typical
cider	gipsy/gypsy
spaghett<u>i</u>	macaron<u>i</u>

CHANGING Y TO I, AND OTHERWISE

buy	buying
enjoy	enjoying
pay	paying
day	daily
lay	laid
pay	paid
say	said
*beauty	beautiful
busy	business

dry	dried
happy	happier
hungry	hungrier
lonely	lonelier
necessary	necessarily
pretty	prettier	prettiest
rely	reliable

CHANGING IE TO Y

die	dying
lie	lying
tie	tying

USE OF C, K, CK, OR S

calendar   capital   climate
collapse

kebab   kennel   kidney   kilometre
kiosk   kitten
kangaroo   karate

cease   ceiling   celery
cellar   cement   centre

century   circle (c used here before i or e)

secretary   second   sentry

solitary   safari   sandwich

sudden (s used here before, a, o or u)

Adding k to c before an ending

panicked   trafficked (ck before e, i or y)

music   musical

mechanic   mechanically

automatic   automatically (c before a or o)

'ck' after short vowels

attack   bucket   package   racket

shocking wicket

-ac or -ic words

Atlantic   historic   lunatic

mechanic   music   Pacific

traffic

kiosk   trek

icicle

MORE BEGINNINGS
ante-/anti- words

ante- = before	anti- = opposite
antemeridiem (a.m.)	anterior
antibiotic	anticlockwise
antiseptic	antitank

em-, en-, in-, im- words

enchant	encircle	enclose
encourage	energy	engage
engine	entertain	enthusiasm
envelope		
embarrass	embrace	emerge
emergency	emotion	emperor
empty		
income	indicate	inland
intelligence	intend	interval
involve		
image	imitate	impact
import	important	impulse

un-, in-, il-, im-, ir- words

unarmed	unasked	unavoidable

unbeliever   uncertain   unbutton

unconscious   undesirable   unfaithful

uneducated   unemployed   unfamiliar

unforgettable   unfortunate

ungenerous

unhealthy   unkind   unpleasant

unreasonable   unreliable

inaccurate   inadequate

inattentive   incapable

inconsistent   independent

indigestible   ineligible

infrequent   innocent

invisible

illegal   illegible   illiterate

immature   immobile   immoral

impatient   imperfect   impolite

impossible   important   impractical

irrational   irregular   irresistible

irreversible

for-/fore- beginnings

forbidden   forcible   forget

forgive   forgotten   forward

forearm   forecast   forehead

foreign   foresight   foretell

foreword

NOTE: 'far-' means 'away or out'
          'fore-' means 'looking to the future' or 'in the
          forefront'.

SILENT BEGINNINGS AND MIDDLES

heir   honest   hour

gnat   gnaw   gnome   knee

kneel   knife   knight   knitting

knock   knot   knowledge knuckle

pneumonia   psychology   pterodactyl

wrap   wreck   wren   wrestle

wriggle   wring   wrinkle   wrist

written   wrong

dungeon   pigeon   surgeon

foreign   reign

unknown

biscuit   buoy   honour   labour

savour

answer   sword